The Fun Run

by Zoë Clarke
illustrated by Janet Cheeseman

OXFORD
UNIVERSITY PRESS

Queen Max was on a fun run.

The queen was quick.

It was raining.

Fat toads sat in the path.

Queen Max put them back in the moat.

A big log fell.

I think I can
pull this log.

Mud was on the path.
The mud was deep and wet.

You will not sink.
I can pick you up.

The path had lots of thick weeds.
It was not fun!

Let me keep the weeds back.
Then you can run.

I see big rocks on the path!

I can push
the rocks off.

Queen Max did not win.

You did fix things.
That was quick thinking!

toads

log

mud

rocks

weeds

Encourage students to use the picture to retell the story.